City of Ṣan'ā'

Nomad and City Exhibition

Edited by James Kirkman

Museum of Mankind
Department of Ethnography of the British Museum
World of Islam Festival 1976

مهرجان العالم الإسلامي
World of Islam Festival Publishing Company Ltd

First published 1976
ISBN 0 905035 14 3 paper
ISBN 0 905035 13 5 cased

Published and produced by the World of Islam Festival Publishing Company Ltd.

Designed by Colin Larkin
Edited by Liz Evora
Measured drawings and photographs by Ronald Lewcock
Set in 12/14pt Monophoto Plantin 110
Printed on 115 gsm Blade coated cartridge

Colour origination: Westerham Press
Filmset by Westerham Press and printed in England by
Westerham Press Ltd., Westerham, Kent.

Front cover: View of city from roof-top.

Back cover: Interior view of a typical upper window in stained glass.

Contents

Acknowledgements 4

Introduction 7

The Market 19

The Mosque 33

The Public Baths 39

The House 47

Costume 67

Selected Exhibits 70

Bibliography 83

Acknowledgements

This exhibition is the joint work of the British Museum and the following members of the University of Cambridge, Professor R. B. Serjeant, Dr Ronald Lewcock, Miss Martha Mundy and Mr Robert Wilson.

The exhibition is indebted for the loan of objects, to the National Museum, Ṣan'ā', Professor R. B. Serjeant, Dr Ronald Lewcock ARIBA, Dr Paolo Costa, Dr Brian Doe and Mrs Doreen Ingrams.

It is a pleasure to acknowledge the help with the exhibition and catalogue which has been given by Qadi Isma'il al-Akwa', Director of Antiquities, Yemen Arab Republic; H.E. Husayn al-'Amri, Deputy Minister of Foreign Affairs, Yemen Arab Republic; H.E. the British Ambassador to the Yemen Arab Republic and Mrs D. C. Carden; Dr Paolo Costa, Father Etienne Renaud, Mrs Sylvia Kennedy, Mr Clive Smith and the British Council, Mr Rex Smith, and Dr Robin Bidwell, Secretary of the Middle East Centre, Cambridge University.

The exhibitors are indebted to the Berne Museum for the loan of their dagger-making exhibit, collected by Professor Walter Dostal. The model of the *samsarah* was made by Mr John McLeod, that of the public bath by Mr Simon Jackson, and the house by Mr Hugh Cullen and Miss Marie-Hélène Jeeves.

All photographs are by Dr Ronald Lewcock, except those on pages 14, 16, 35 (R. B. Serjeant), page 31 (Walter Dostal), and pages 60, 66, 69 and coloured plates 9 and 11 (Martha Mundy).

The subjects mentioned in the catalogue will be treated in greater depth in the forthcoming study of Ṣan'ā': *Ṣan'ā' – an Arabian Islamic City*, to be published by the Festival of Islam Trust.

Exhibition design by the British Museum Design Office.

Transliteration is in accordance with the system of *Arabian Studies*.

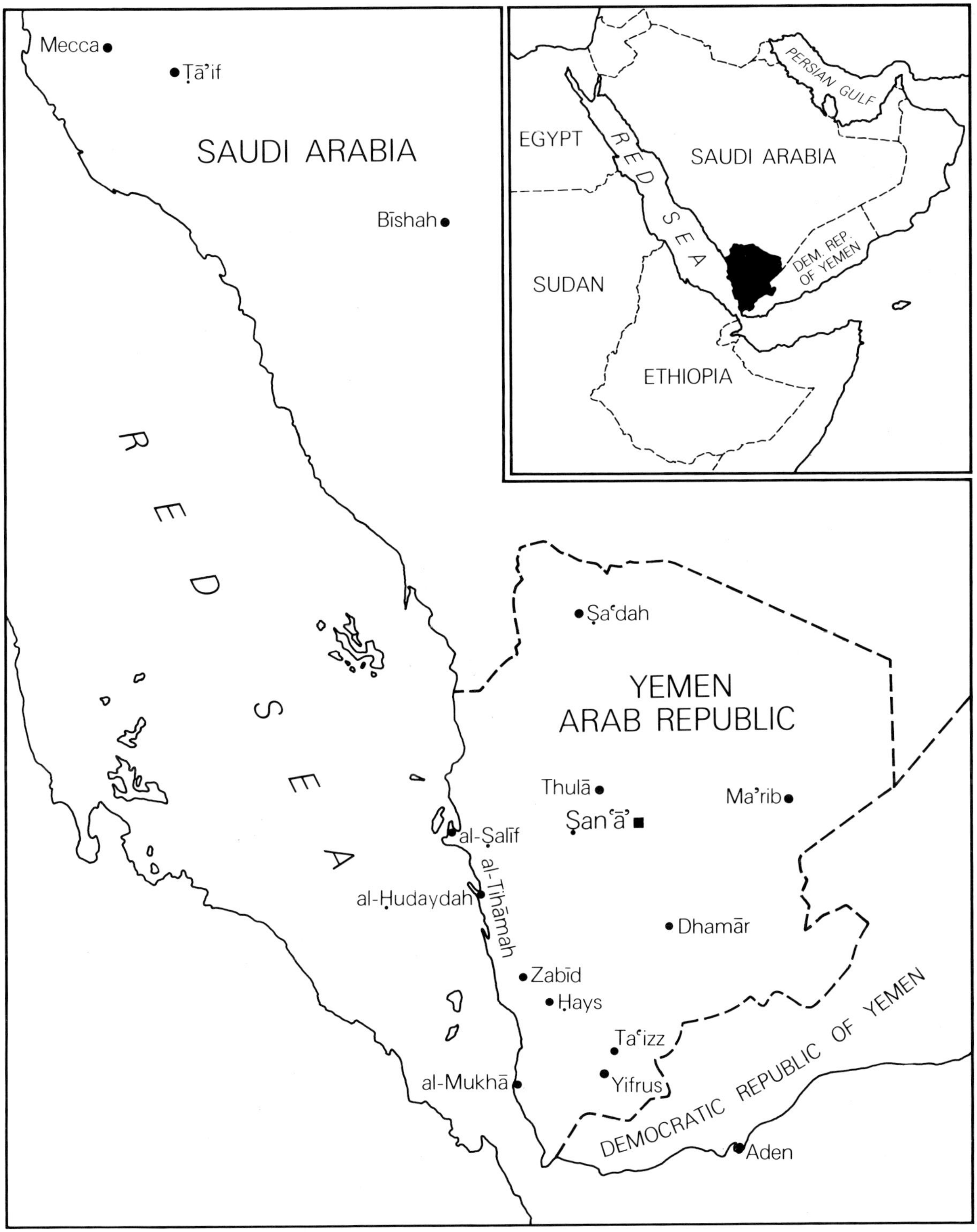
Mecca
Ṭā'if
SAUDI ARABIA
Bīshah
RED SEA
EGYPT
SAUDI ARABIA
PERSIAN GULF
RED SEA
SUDAN
DEM. REP. OF YEMEN
ETHIOPIA
Ṣaʿdah
YEMEN ARAB REPUBLIC
Thulā
Ṣanʿā'
Ma'rib
al-Ṣalīf
al-Tihāmah
al-Ḥudaydah
Dhamār
Zabīd
Ḥays
Taʿizz
Yifrus
al-Mukhā
DEMOCRATIC REPUBLIC OF YEMEN
Aden

Aerial photograph of the city of Ṣan'ā' (photo: Aero-Precisa, Beirut).

Introduction

The Yemen Arab Republic is the southern end of the lofty and rugged mountain range that extends along the western side of Arabia rising from the coastal plain, the Tihāmah, along the Red Sea littoral. It borders with the People's Democratic Republic of South Yemen (the former Aden Protectorate), and on the north and east with Sa'ūdī Arabia. The city of Ṣan'ā' is its northern capital – one of the best-preserved traditional types of Islamic city in the Arabian peninsula, retaining its mediaeval aspect and much of its traditional organization.

The oldest part of Ṣan'ā' is the citadel at its eastern extremity along with al-Qaṭī' district immediately west and south of it on the higher ground. Its large market or *sūq* with its shops and caravanserais lies in a depression that probably, at one time, marked the edge of the city but is now well in the middle of it. During the Islamic period the city extended to al-Sā'ilah, the large watercourse that now bisects it running from south to north, and, in the Ayyūbid age, towards the end of the twelfth century, it extended west of that to form the Bustān al-Sulṭān quarter. The Jewish community, which formerly lived on the eastern bank of the watercourse, was expelled in the seventeenth century and took up residence further west still, in Bīr al-'Azab village. Both Ṣan'ā' and Bīr al-'Azab were surrounded by an adobe wall and linked by gates in the area of the present Mutawakkil Mosque, until this part was demolished after 1962. Between the two and to the south lies the big Khuzaymah Cemetery, now partly built over.

The history of Ṣan'ā' is long and varied. It may have had a certain holy status in the pre-Islamic age, with a sacred area, and it had a splendid castle of many storeys near the present Friday Mosque. Not long before Islam, the Abyssinian conquerors of the Yemen built a church there, al-Qalīs (*ecclesia*), the site of which is still shown to visitors. Towards the end of the sixth century a Persian expedition which arrived from the Gulf by sea numbered Ṣan‘ā’ among its conquests. These Persians intermarried locally, and for some centuries the city was divided between these Arabicized Persians and the Arab Banū Shibhāb tribe. It was with these Persian rulers, the Abnā’, that the Prophet's emissaries dealt when Islam was introduced to the Yemen.

As late as the ninth century we still hear of a Bishop of Ṣan‘ā’, but the Christians were probably absorbed in the Muslim community. The Jews, however, remained a separate community, forming in the present century nearly a quarter of the inhabitants. They were mostly artisans, though of course there were Arab artisans as well, and Ṣan‘ā’ was basically a centre of Arab-Islamic civilization. Most of the Jews left Ṣan‘ā’ in 1949–50, but the ruler of the Yemen, Imām Aḥmad, insisted that they should instruct Muslims to replace them in the special crafts they practised.

The most ancient Islamic monument still extant is the Great Mosque, the Jāmi‘, founded by command of the Prophet Muḥammad and constructed beside Ghumdān Castle in the garden of one of the Persian governors. Ghumdān, long destroyed, lies under a great artificial mound near the Great Mosque. The mosque itself has built into it some pre-Islamic inscriptions in 'Ḥimyar' characters.

Islamic Yemen was first ruled by governors sent from Medina, but after the capital of Islam moved to Damascus, in A.D. 661, the Umayyad caliphs, now rulers of Islam, appointed governors to Ṣan‘ā’, as did their successors, the ‘Abbāsid caliphs, with their capital at Baghdad. These governors usually seem to have been local Yemeni nominees, but they remitted taxes to Baghdad while it still retained some control over the province. One of these ‘Abbāsid governors, was responsible for leading water into Ṣan‘ā’ by an underground channel called after him, al-Barmakī. This provided water for Ṣan‘ā’ for many centuries.

The Prophet's cousin, ‘Alī, husband of his daughter

View from a high *mafraj* (room for entertainment) in the city.

The western part of the old city from the air, showing the tower houses that line the narrow streets, and the large market gardens behind them.

Fāṭimah, had never really acquiesced to the succession of others than himself to the caliphate, and his descendants considered themselves to be the legitimate leaders or imāms of the Islamic state. Consequently risings of these 'Alī-ids against the caliphs were frequent. One of these 'Alī-ids, who sought his fortune through carving out an Islamic state of his own from the vast 'Abbāsid Empire, was al-Hādī ilā 'l-Ḥaqq (the Guide to the Truth), at about the close of the ninth century. He founded a dynasty at Ṣa'dah, a town several days' journey north of Ṣan'ā'. These 'Alī-ids are called Zaydīs after an ancestor who met his death in a rising against the Umayyad caliphs. Al-Hādī held Ṣan'ā' only briefly. He was dislodged by a native Yemeni dynasty, the Yu'firids. The latter in turn had to combat an extremist sect, the Qarmaṭīs, believed to have tried to undermine Islamic society by attacking its morals, especially in the matters of sexual restraint, the prohibition of drinking wine and licentiousness in general. The leader

A group of tall houses near the principal wadi that runs through the city.

of this group, which had relations with the Fāṭimid rulers of Egypt, is said to have made a sort of bath above a wing of the Great Mosque which leaked and damaged its beautiful painted wooden ceiling!

In the succeeding centuries various dynasties rose to prominence in the Yemen, but the Zaydīs in the north remained relatively constant, their fortunes varying so that they sometimes held Ṣan'ā', sometimes not. The picture is confused by endless wars and battles. The Ṣulayḥids and Hamdān Sulṭāns, the latter from one of the most powerful tribes in the Ṣan'ā' region, gave way to the Ayyūbids, a dynasty founded by the celebrated Saladin, who invaded the Yemen. In Ṣan'ā' they built palaces west of al-Sā'ilah. They gave way to the Rasūlids, whose capital was at Ta'izz, though they held Ṣan'ā' intermittently. They gave the Yemen one of its most settled periods of rule and were not only fine builders but men of literature and science. However they in turn were overcome by the Ṭāhirids, who captured Ṣan'ā' and filled in the underground water channels.

The Ṭāhirid dynasty, met its end at the hands of invaders – the Egyptian Mamlūks, who had reacted to the Portuguese entry into the Indian Ocean, and to Albuquerque's attempt to capture Aden in 1513, by dispatching a fleet down the Red Sea; this fleet also mounted an invasion of the Lower Yemen. Their well-organized troops defeated the Ṭāhirids in battle, in part because they used firearms against them for the first time in Yemeni history. Meanwhile the Ottoman Turks of Constantinople defeated the Mamlūks of Egypt, but they continued their policy of struggling against the Portuguese in the Indian Ocean.

The Zaydī imām who now ruled Ṣan'ā' again had taken advantage of the Mamlūk defeat of the Ṭāhirids, and their subsequent weakness, to reduce the last shreds of Ṭāhirid influence; but when the Ottomans appeared on the scene he withdrew to the north. Jealousies within the imāmī house made it possible for the Ottoman Turks to enter and sack Ṣan'ā', which had been treacherously delivered to them by a Yemeni who admitted them through the entrances at the Sā'ilah watercourse. During the century or so of Ottoman occupation each Turkish governor tried to depart with a fortune at the end of his term of office, though the Ottomans did leave some notable achievements, such as the registration of the properties of the *waqf* (religious endowment) of the country and construction of the Bakīriyyah Mosque and others in Ṣan'ā'. Nevertheless the Yemenis hated and feared them for their cruelty and rapacity, and despite their military successes, greater than those of any subsequent invaders, the Ottomans found that the Yemen swallowed up men and treasure, yet remained turbulent and unsettled.

The Zaydī imām, al-Qāsim the Great, who revived Yemeni opposition to the Ottomans, is respected as the founder of the present Zaydī dynasty. His son, al-Mu'ayyad, largely completed the process of expelling the Ottoman forces, but it was the Imām al-Mutawakkil who extended imāmī rule to the furthest limits it ever reached, sending expeditions which subjugated Ḥaḍramawt and the tribes south of the present Yemen Arab Republic.

In the following centuries the Zaydī imāms, many of whom did not reside at Ṣan'ā' but in some fortified mountain village, were unable to maintain control of all this extensive territory, which was broken up by steep mountains or steppe. The death of an imām almost invariably brought a dispute over his successor. A strong imām would bring the tribes to heel, maintain security on the roads, collect taxes and benefit the country in general. Warring imāms supported by tribal factions created anarchy. Ṣan'ā', set on its high mountain plain, was not greatly affected by events in the outside world, though it was aware of them, but it was sensitive to every local tribal movement. Visits by Europeans from Mocha, like those made by Sir Henry Middleton and many other westerners, if not ignored by the Yemeni historians, are given at best a mere line or two in the chronicles.

By the nineteenth century the rule of the imāms was falling into confusion, and the Ottoman Turks were once more bent on extending imperial rule in Arabia. In 1872 they took Ṣan'ā' and set up a Turkish administration in the Yemen. Once again the occupation proved to be a drain on Ottoman manpower. The Yemenis reacted to Turkish exactions and harshness. In the mountains the Zaydīs rallied round a new imām, Yaḥyā al-Mutawakkil, of the Ḥamīd al-Dīn house. The tribes besieged Ṣan'ā', which fell to them in 1905, though the Turks later retook it. Another siege in 1911 by the imām, though the city was not taken, convinced the Turks that they must come to an understanding with the imām – which they did, conceding in substance to all his demands. The Ṣan'ānīs criticized the Turks for drinking openly and for their immorality, but respected them as soldiers. Indeed there are traces of Turkish influence in Ṣan'ā' even today, and such buildings as the barracks to the south stand as a reminder of their presence.

After the First World War Imām Yaḥyā entered Ṣan'ā' amid acclamations from the citizens. He had virtually to conquer certain provinces of what now constitutes the Yemen Arab Republic. Though successful in establishing law and order, as well as extending traditional education, repairing mosques and constructing some roads, Imām Yaḥyā was conservative and isolationist. His habit of hoarding money against emergencies gained him the reputation of miserliness, and the traditional fiscal system bore hard on the southern districts. In 1948 he was murdered outside Ṣan'ā' by members of a conspiracy headed by 'Abdullāh al-Wazīr, who belonged to a prominent Sayyid family that had helped him to power, only to be cast aside by him. This rising was against Yaḥyā, not the Imāmate.

The conspirators failed, however, to assassinate his able and vigorous son, Crown Prince Aḥmad, at Ta'izz, and he roused the northern tribes to capture Ṣan'ā'. They were permitted to sack the town by way of reward. Many prosperous merchant families were ruined as a result and the great caravanserai or *samsarah* of Muḥammad b. Ḥasan, founded centuries earlier, has been closed from that day to this.

Imām Aḥmad's tremendous personality held the Yemen together, and he scotched a number of conspiracies, even those in which his own brothers were involved, winning the sometimes unwilling admiration of the Yemenis. But the Imāmī family was divided within itself; subversive influences from abroad had begun to penetrate the country, and the many Yemenis working in Aden had before their eyes the contrast of the growth of Aden's prosperity and their own country's backwardness. All of this led to dissatisfaction with the regime. Imām

Typical tribesmen from Khawlān.

Aḥmad's son al-Badr, the heir apparent, resided in Ṣan'ā', where he built himself a mansion, Dār al-Bashāyir. To counter his uncle's ambitions, which were supported by conservative northern groups, he tried to win the younger army officers and 'youth' by aligning himself with Nasser of Egypt. During his father's latter years he was instrumental in obtaining foreign aid for development; the Chinese, for instance, constructed the modern road from al-Ḥudaydah port to Ṣan'ā'.

Al-Badr was paid allegiance as imām on his father's death in 1962, but within a week his mansion was attacked by a young officer group with tanks. Al-Badr put up a spirited resistance, then left Ṣan'ā' to rally the tribes, undergoing many adventures *en route*. Nasser sent large forces to support the officers' *coup d'état*, and these forces occupied much of the Yemen until the June War of 1967, when they had to withdraw. Since then the Yemen Arab Republic has come into its own, with Ṣan'ā' as the seat of government.

The Yemen is an agricultural country producing grain, fruit (notably grapes) and the *qāt* leaf; it rears sheep and some cattle. The population consists mainly of tribal farmers, and the few large towns are basically markets for the exchange of country products for local or imported manufactured goods. The two main ports are al-Ḥudaydah and al-Mukhā (Mocha). The tribesmen under their elected shaykhs are often almost independent of central governments. Under their protection live many Sayyid families, descendants of the Prophet. The hereditary Qāḍī class with the Sayyids form a learned aristocracy, are the representatives of Islam, act as mediators and are often employed as government officials. The imāms of the Yemen were themselves drawn from the larger Sayyid families. Since 1962 their pre-eminent position has diminished, especially in the large towns, and the younger generation of Sayyids often prefers to ignore its prophetic descent. Ṣan'ā' itself is said to be traditionally protected by seven great northern tribal confederations, though this protection has often been violated. Yet Ṣan'ā', as the market for many tribes, is neutral ground for them, and they cannot pursue their blood feuds within its walls.

The citizens of Ṣan'ā' include many Sayyids and

Qāḍīs; those engaged in business are well represented in the cloth markets, Sūq al-Fitlah and Sūq al-Kawāfī, but many craftsmen and traders probably originated from tribal families and are settled in Ṣan'ā'. Some crafts are regarded in Ṣan'ā' as occupations in which a man may honourably be engaged – for example the making of weapons, water-pipes and plaster windows, or masonry, brick-laying and dyeing. On the other hand it is socially demeaning to engage in any kind of leather work, or be in attendance on the human body – such as barbers, bathmen

'*Āqil* (headman of a quarter).

and coffee-house keepers – or to be a butcher or a *qashshām*, who attends to the mosque gardens. These last are called the Banī Khums. The Jews were silversmiths at the top end of their own social scale, at the lowest end, scavengers. As silversmiths they were in charge of the Mint.

Like all southern Arabian towns, Ṣan'ā' is divided into quarters. Each quarter is administered by elected headmen, who maintain security and collect taxes and imposts. Each craft has a shaykh, a sort of headman who keeps an eye on prices and trade practices, and these shaykhs elect the Shaykh al-Mashāyikh as the head shaykh of the market. As in other Yemenite cities, Ṣan'ā' Market maintains an elaborate system of night-watchmen under the 'Shaykh of the Night', and they keep guard from their little brick cabins on the roofs of shops. A municipality (*baladiyyah*) was set up during the second Ottoman Turk occupation and this has taken over some of the traditional services of the city.

R. B. Serjeant

Rulers of the northern Yemen

These dates are only approximate, as dynasties and rulers often overlap, and the Zaydī imāms have sometimes ruled most of the Yemen and sometimes been refugees in the mountains.

Governors of the Prophet, Umayyad and 'Abbāsid dynasties	early seventh century-847
Yu'firids	847–998
Zaydī imāms of Ṣa'dah	*c.* 896
Ṣulayḥids	1037–88
Sulṭāns of Hamdān	1099–1173
Ayyūbids	1173–1229
Rasūlids (Ta'izz)	1229–1454
Ṭāhirids	1454–1526
Mamlūks	1511–21
First Ottoman occupation	1536–1636
Zaydī imāms	*c.* 1630–*c.* 1872
Second Ottoman occupation	*c.* 1872–1918
Zaydī imāms	1918
Yemen Arab Republic	1962

Panorama of Ṣan'ā' market. The high buildings are caravanserais (*samsarahs*) and the low roofs cover market stalls.

The Market

Ṣan'ā' market or *sūq* is located in the heart of the present city, and each craft or trade has its own street or area and appears to have occupied the same site for centuries. A craft elects its own shaykhs or headmen, who elect a chief shaykh of the market. The shaykhs decide the craft regulations and fix a fair price for the articles sold. Until lorry transport took over, camels, mules and donkeys used to come direct to the Warehouse of the Scales (Samsarat al-Mīzān) in the centre of the market, where their loads would be taxed; a tax was also levied on animals brought into the city. Goods were then transferred to the other *samsarahs*, most of which were inns as well as stores. Goods were moved to and from the warehouses on the backs of porters.

A *samsarah* is a multi-storeyed structure. On the ground floor are stables and storerooms, with sometimes a mezzanine floor reached by a wooden staircase; above, there is a series of rooms for lodging and storing goods, opening off an open court with arcaded loggias constructed over the buildings of the first court. Separate staircases lead to different parts of the upper storeys. At the entrance a room is provided for the guards of the warehouses, who control the admission and removal of all goods and receive the dues to be paid. The *samsarahs* are owned by the mosques.

Dates for the building of the *samsarahs* and the other structures in the *sūq* are difficult to establish. The method of construction, stonework laced with large wooden baulks of timber, of parts of the *sūq* and Samsarat al-Baw'ānī shows that these walls may be the oldest structures surviving in Ṣan'ā'. The Samsarat al-Mīzān (the Warehouse of the Scales) may be as old as the seventh/fourteenth century, while the Samsarat al-Majjah is said to have been in use for more than three hundred years.

This warehouse is typical of the warehouses of Ṣan'ā'. On the street there are a number of shops, flanking the entrance, which is slightly off-centre. A wide passage leads into the building past the guard's room, where he often smokes a water-pipe while watching the loading and unloading of goods. The passage opens into a high central stable area, with a roof supported by a central row of three columns from a pre-Islamic building. It is surrounded on four sides by storerooms on two levels, those on the mezzanine floor reached by a flight of steps at the far end. Top lights in the ceiling give adequate illumination.

Opposite the entrance passage a broad doorway opens into a second stable, larger and higher than the other. The roof is supported by a tall central column and a surrounding colonnade; access to the upper levels is provided by a staircase at one end. Above there are two central courts open to the sky; each is surrounded by rooms, three levels in one court and two in the other; these were, until recently, used almost entirely for living

Typical scene in the market centre. Tribesmen come in from the surrounding plains and mountains, or from the distant coast.

The lowest levels of the caravanserai are occupied by stables for animals, surrounded by small storerooms for goods.

accommodation for travelling merchants and their retainers. Today the old patterns of trade have been destroyed; the top floors of the big warehouses are hardly used and are rapidly crumbling through neglect.

The Samsarat al-Majjah is constructed in stone to the top of the stables and above in burnt brick. A splendid triple arch motif has been used to accentuate the entrance, and the large blank areas have been relieved by brick-work patterns which are repeated on the wide arches framing the first row of rooms on the roof.

The shops in each part of the market normally sell only closely allied lines of stock. They consist of a counter with a shallow space behind, seldom more than 3 metres square and sometimes as small as $1\frac{1}{2}$ metres, and a limited area for storage, which is even more restricted when crafts have to be carried on in it. Six stalls have been reconstructed for the exhibition:

1 stall for coffee husk, raisins and almonds
2 stall for grain (sorghum, wheat, barley) and pulses (peas, beans, lentils)
3 stall for spices
4 stall for perfumes
5 stall for daggers
6 stall for pottery, bowls and jugs

Raisins, pulses and small quantities of coffee husk are sold by volume and measured in wooden containers (*qadaḥ*) marked with the name of the imām ruling when the measure was certified, and sometimes with a symbol indicating volume. When the imām died the name of the new imām was added; some *qadaḥs* have the names of as many as three imāms: al-Mutawakkil, al-Manṣūr and al-Mahdī. The units are the *qadaḥ* and the *nafar*, which was $\frac{1}{64}$th of a *qadaḥ*. The measures in general use are the $\frac{1}{8}$th of a *qadaḥ* and the $\frac{1}{16}$th of a *qadaḥ*, commonly called the '$\frac{1}{2}$ of an $\frac{1}{8}$th', and the $\frac{1}{4}$, 1 and 2 *nafar*. The *qadaḥ* is approximately 36 litres.

The principal grain foods in Ṣan'ā' are wheat and sorghum, which are sold in woollen sacks (*ghirārāh*) embellished with bands of black and pink thread on a white ground or of white on a black ground. The sacks vary in size from 13 by 72 centimetres to 63 by 120 centimetres. Coffee husk, sugar, nuts and meat are also

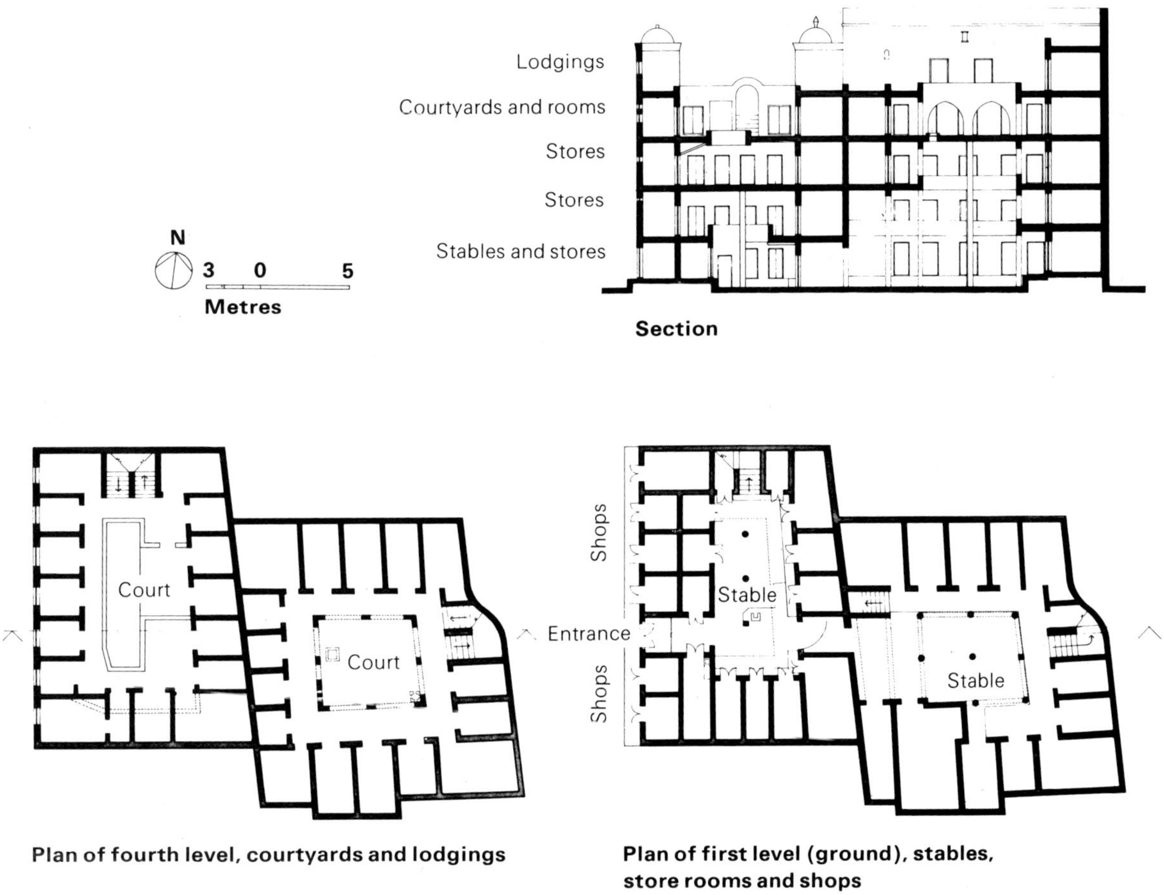

Plan and section of Samsarat al-Majjah, a typical *samsarah*, (model in exhibition).

normally sold by weight, and are weighed on a bronze steelyard gradated on a duodecimal system. The steelyard carries a tray (diameter 8 centimetres) beside the hook for measuring small quantities.

Arabia is a land of spices, and a list of those sold in the market would include: turmeric (*hurud*); pepper (*filfil*); cumin (*kammūn*); cardamom (*hayl*), probably from India; cloves (*zirr*); fenugreek (*ḥilbah*); coriander (two varieties, *nakhwah* and *kabzarah*); fennel (*shumār/shamār*); thyme (*za'tar*); cinnamon (*qirfah*); tamarind (*tamar Hindī*); ginger (*zinjabīl*); garlic (*thūmah*); 'water' incense (*bukhūr mā'*), used for perfuming water flasks; and *ḥutum*, a potash made from burning a plant called '*aṣal*, which is used with *shādhar* (unidentified) and henna, pounded together to dye the hair and nails. They are

General view of street of market stalls.

Samsarat al-Majjah, front view.

weighed on scales, using a system based on the *ūqiyyah* or ounce, which is the weight of a Maria Theresa dollar. The number of *ūqiyyah* to the *raṭl* (pound) varies according to the commodity in which dealings are taking place.

The perfumery shops sell most of the spices, and in addition a variety of substances including galingale, galls, asafoetida, aloes, ambergris, civet, musk, indigo, madder, and a number of compounds which have a medicinal use. These are described in a book of drugs composed by a Yemeni monarch in the late thirteenth century.

Salt is brought in woollen bags from open-cast workings in the interior near Ma'rib, and from similar workings on the coast near Ṣalīf. It is sold at the spices stall in bags made of plaited palm fronds holding about 5 *raṭl*.

The inner stables, surrounded by storerooms on three levels, of Samsarat al-Majjah.

Local craftsmanship has diminished over the last twenty years in the face of competition from cheap imported goods, and many crafts have disappeared. Nevertheless, the manufacture of fine daggers continues. The tanged blades are on average 8 centimetres wide at the hilt and 40 to 50 centimetres long, and are slightly curved. The hilts are of bone or horn. The scabbard is made of two slats of wood covered with leather. Belts are of brocaded cotton with metallic threads. There are two main types of dagger. One is worn as an article of costume and has a small crescent-shaped pommel, often decorated, as is the scabbard, with elaborate patterns of silver thread and silver granular work; the other is utilitarian and has a simple hilt and a T-shaped pommel to ensure a firm grip.

Bowls and jugs are made on a mould in a pink earthenware with a slip and decorated with random bands of a reddish mineral paint (*mishk*). A rough yellow-brown or green glazed ware is imported from Ḥays on the Tihāmah (coastal plain) for sale in the market.

Also sold in the market are baskets, trays for winnowing grain or displaying spices and *makhbazahs* (pillow-like objects used in bread-making. The plain basket surface is relieved by strands of red, blue and green.

In the building trade the crafts of the mason, the carpenter and ironsmith flourish. The windows made of imported coloured glass set in gypsum plaster tracery are characteristic of the houses of Ṣan'ā'.

Stall selling coffee husk (*qishr*), used for making Yemeni coffee, and coffee beans.

Stall selling raisins and almonds.

Stall selling spices.

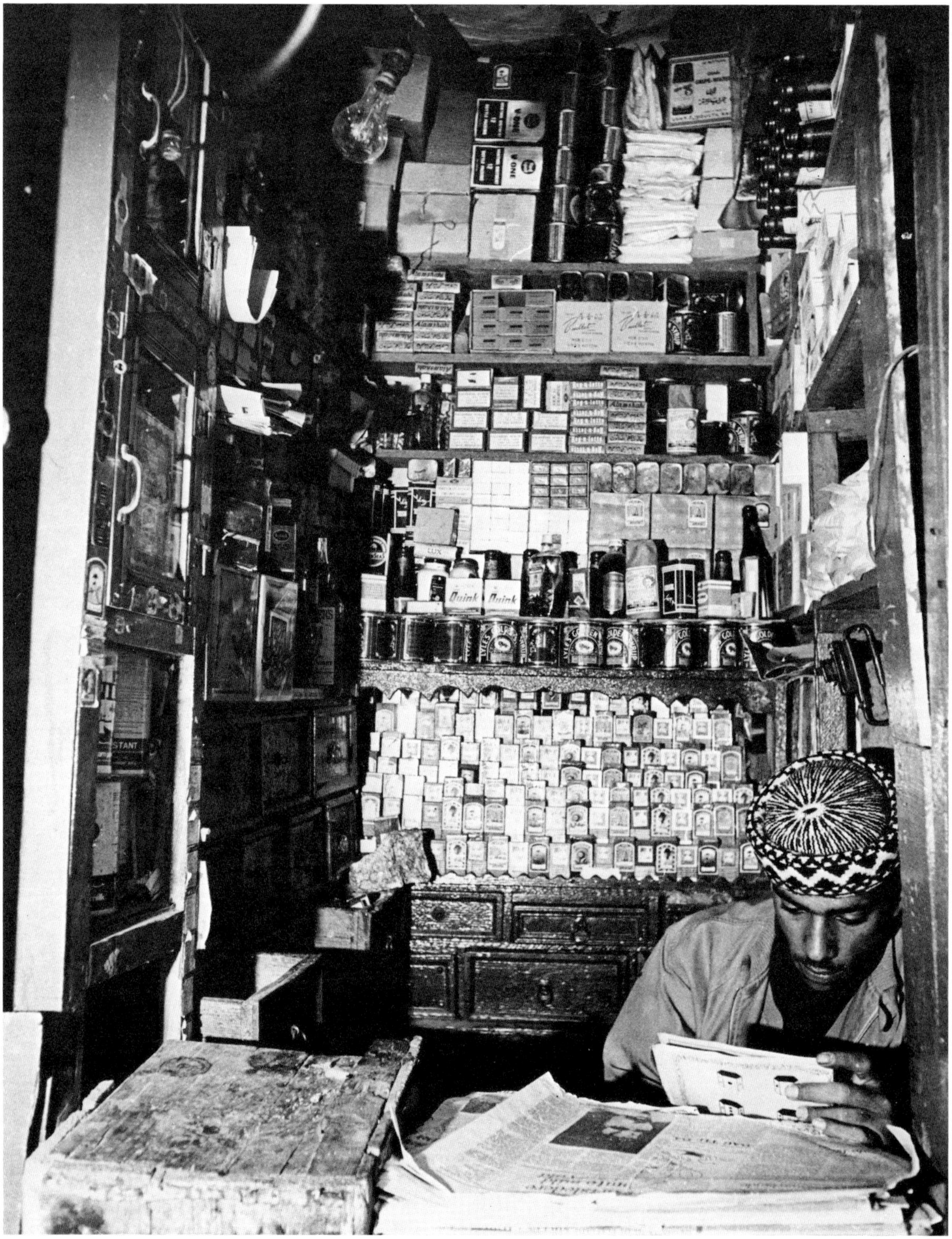

Stall selling perfumes, *'atars* and medicinal herbs.

Man making dagger scabbard.

Man making dagger.

Great Mosque, aerial view.

Plate 1. View of city at Ṭalḥah, Qubbat Ṭalḥah in foreground.

Plate 2. Typical market garden, with minarets of Great Mosque in background.

Plate 3. Market garden with large houses in background. The model in the exhibition is based on the house in the centre.

Plate 4. Lower reception room in a house, showing traditional furnishings and alabaster upper windows, with a Ṣanʿā' family eating their midday meal.

Plate 5. Woman's full '*uṣbah* head-dress.

Plate 6. Group of women wearing the traditional Ṣan'ā' cloak (*sitārah*). The modern iron doors are made and painted in Ṣan'ā'.

Plate 7. Two shop-keepers from Ṣan'ā' market relaxing in a *mafraj*. In the foreground is a bundle of goods wrapped in a shoulder cloth.

Plate 8. Tribesman wearing shoulder cloth and a dagger with rhinoceros horn hilt.

Plate 9. Unmarried girl wearing shawl (*fūlah*) above the indoor veil (*lithmah*); under the shawl she has a bonnet (*qarqūsh*) embroidered in silver thread.

Plate 10. Tribesman in traditional dress: an indigo turban on his head; a full-length robe (*qamīṣ*) with wide sleeves tied up behind his back; shoulder cloth (*liḥfah*); dagger with rhinoceros horn hilt (*ʿasīb*); and a second (white) cloth. Behind the dagger in his belt is a sprig of sweet basil (*rayḥān*), an aromatic plant.

Plate 11. Initial stages in dressing a girl in the *tashbīk* head-dress. The woman in blue is a professional marriage dresser (*shāriʿah*).

Plate 12. Room for entertainment (*mafraj*) in a large house.

The Mosque

The tribesman admits superiority only to men endowed with the gift of religion, but religion comes from the city, not from the steppe. An Arabian prophet of personality, integrity and political wisdom can sometimes unite the warring tribes. The greatest of all Arabian men of religion was the Prophet Muḥammad, founder of Islam, born at Mecca in the late sixth century A.D. of an aristocratic family among whom were the hereditary custodians of the temple of Ka'bah.

Muḥammad's preaching of the One God, Allāh, conflicted with the interests of the pagan lords of Mecca and in A.D. 622, the year of the Hijra, from which the Muslim era is dated, he left Mecca and sought the protection of the tribes of Yathrib in the town later called Medina, the City of the Prophet. Their chiefs accepted the doctrine of Islam: that there is one God Allāh and that Muḥammad is his Prophet. Over the next eleven years Muḥammad, by his political genius and military expeditions, obtained control of Mecca and most of Arabia.

The rulers of Ṣan'ā' were descended from Persians who had arrived as conquerors in the sixth century A.D., had intermarried with the Yemenis and formed an important section of the population. They made an agreement with the Prophet and Islam was introduced into Ṣan'ā'.

Muḥammad's inspired utterances were collected in the Muslim sacred book, al-Qur'ān al-Karīm, which is regarded by Muslims as the literal word of God and is recited at certain hours of the day all over the Muslim world, always in Arabic, for Islam is an Arabian religion and the Qur'ān is an Arabian book. The 'Traditions' record the Prophet's words, actions and judgements, but the complex system of Islamic law and theology was developed by professional scholars, the '*ulamā*', in the great capitals of the Islamic world. There also, and from many sources, was formed the intellectual and material culture we all recognize as Islamic.

The mosque is the place of prayer demanded by Islamic ritual, and the Islamic community is required to attend the 'Friday prayer' at noon each week. This is an expression of its religious and, in early days, of its political unity. The basic requirement is an open court for use in hot weather and a sheltered room in cold weather. As ritual cleanliness is a necessary preliminary to prayer, mosques are provided with ablution places, which today form a conspicuous part of the precincts. A niche in the wall, called the *miḥrāb* or *qiblah*, indicates the direction of Mecca, to which the Muslim turns to pray. The call to prayer was originally made from the roof of the mosque, and the early Zaydī Imāms prohibited minarets, the towers from which the call to prayer was later given. However, minarets are now a striking feature of the Ṣan'ā' skyline and have often been added to mosques which formerly had none.

There are about a hundred mosques in Ṣan'ā', of which thirty-four are large and of some age, and two were built recently. Many of the remainder are small and are associated with the city quarters. Of the early mosques, three are known to contain considerable architectural remains of their early construction. These are the Great Mosque, the Jabbānnah, which is outside the walls and really a place of prayer for the two great feasts, and the Farwah b. Musayk Mosque, all earlier than the fourth/tenth century.

The Great Mosque is substantially the rebuilding of *c.* 87/705 by order of the Caliph al-Walīd, in which the original mosque ordered by the Prophet was greatly enlarged, making use of old Islamic and pre-Islamic material. In 262/875 the mosque was severely damaged by a flood, and it suffered again when Ṣan'ā' was sacked by the Qarmaṭīs in 299/911. An important restoration, including magnificent wooden ceilings, was carried out by Queen Arwā bint Aḥmad in 525/1130–1. The eastern minaret appears to have been in existence at the time of the Qarmaṭī attack; the western was apparently added later. Both were restored in the seventh/thirteenth century.

Apart from the three mentioned above, a number of mosques are cited by Islamic historians as foundations of the early centuries of Islam. They conform to a general type, which comprises a large prayer hall with a flat roof supported on tall columns, approached through a courtyard, on one side of which are open-air ablutions. An enclosed ablution room is also sometimes provided. The reconstructed mosque in the exhibition is an example of the prayer hall of this type of mosque, the *qiblah* wall being a reproduction of the ninth/fifteenth-century wall of the early mosque of Ṭāwūs, with the addition of a recessed *minbar* which does not exist in the original building.

During the first Turkish occupation a number of mosques were built, including the Qubbat Ṭalḥah, which is typical of a small mosque in the Ottoman style, built in the early eleventh/seventeenth century on an old mosque site of the same name.

Great Mosque, north prayer hall.

The mosque functions as a centre for study and teaching, and to this the Arab author Amīn Riḥānī, writing in the early 1930s, attributes the small degree of illiteracy he found in Ṣan'ā'. Ṣan'ā' was also a city of learning, and students, called *muhājirūn*, came from outside and resided in a row of cells close to the Jāmi' Mosque, where recently a hoard of very early Qur'ānic and other manuscripts was discovered.

The Yemenis are divided between the 'legitimists', Shī'ah Zaydīs, supporters of the claims of the house of 'Alī to the Imāmate, in the north and the Sunnī Shāfi'is in the south, but in practice there is no great cleavage between them. They pray in the same mosques and a member of either sect may act as Imām Miḥrāb Ṣan'ā', or the leader in prayer. There are also small communities of Ismā'īlīs. During their two occupations the Ottomans encouraged the Sunnī Ḥanafīs.

There is little furniture in the mosque. The pulpit (*minbar*) is in the form of a seat, approached by a flight of steps, made of wood and elaborately decorated. There will often be a book-rest to hold the Qur'ān and a cupboard for books.

Lighting was by oil lamps burning sesame oil, or candles. Electricity has now taken their place to a great extent.

The floor is covered with carpets, on which the congregation kneels to pray in the prescribed manner. Some of the carpets are of local manufacture, such as those with black stripes on a white ground (*Dhamār*), about 1 metre wide and varying in length from 1.7 to 3.9 metres; another type (*al-Ṭā'if*) with multi-coloured stripes, 74 centimetres wide and about 3.3 metres long, which are often sewn together to cover a broader area, is imported from Sa'ūdī Arabīa.

Qubbat Ṭalḥah, view from above.

Ḥammām Shukr, entrance.

The Public Baths

Ṣan'ā' has a hot, dusty climate and the baths are used by almost everyone once a week. Within the city there are eighteen public baths, which are run by hereditary bath-keepers who charge a small fee for their use.

The plan of the baths is unlike that of the baths of Cairo, Syria or Turkey, and resembles the baths of the later Roman Empire in Libya as regards the system of heating and the grouping together of a number of small rooms for the hot and temperate zones. From the architecture it would appear that the two oldest baths are the Yāsir and Shukr, which differ from the others by the absence of the central pool in the cool room. This distinction is supported by local tradition, which considers Yāsir to be the oldest, followed by Shukr. The Ḥammām al-Maydān was built in 1007/1598, the Ḥammām al-Sulṭān a hundred years later.

Fuel for the baths is seldom wood, which is scarce. Instead two alternatives are used. The first is the refuse of skins and bones from the slaughter yards, the second is human excrement. This is collected from the small chamber built for the purpose at the bottom of the 'long-drop' latrine in every house, and is spread on the roof of the baths or in the yard behind, which is often at a level with the roof, to dry. After burning, the ash is taken away and sold as fertilizer for the orchards and vegetable gardens.

The yard behind the baths contains the well and the reservoirs, from which water is drawn as required through either the hot boiler or the cold reservoir immediately adjacent to the bath. There is a system of pipes carrying both hot and cold water to the hot and temperate rooms.

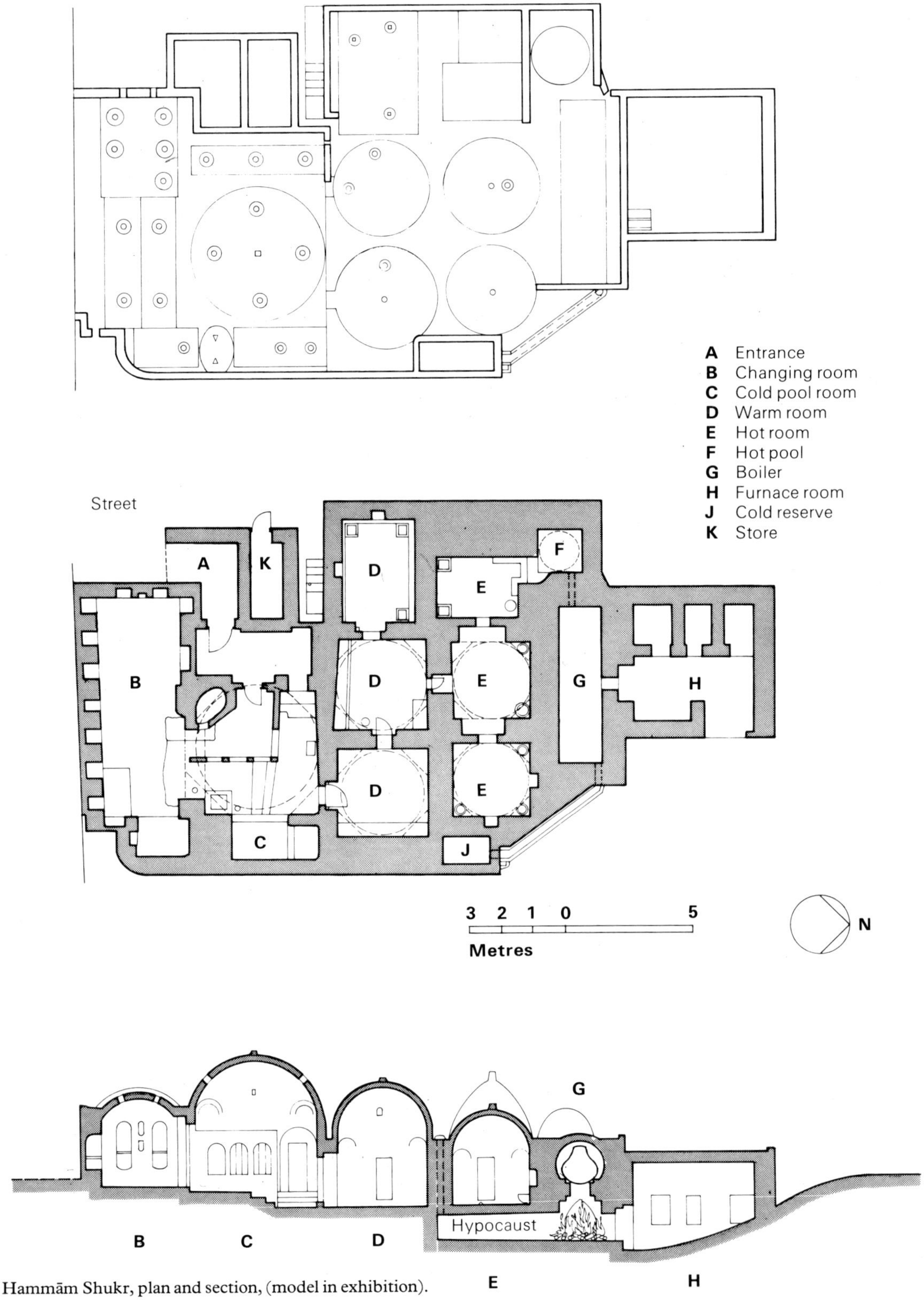

Hammām Shukr, plan and section, (model in exhibition).

Most baths are open four days a week for men and three for women. On Friday all the baths are open for men. Some baths open more often for women than for men, because the women remain longer and pay more. The baths are usually available for eighteen hours, from four in the morning until ten at night, and closed for the remaining few hours. The fires have to be lit two hours before opening time.

The rooms which make up the hot area have floors heated by hypocausts and walls by vertical flues; two-thirds of each bath is below ground level to conserve heat. The warm rooms are in two zones; a temperate zone of three rooms and a hot one of three similar rooms.

On entering, the bather leaves his valuables with the keeper of the baths, takes off his garments and puts on a cloth (*fūṭah*) which he has brought with him. He then goes down the steps leading from the changing room to the bath proper. He proceeds straight through the temperate rooms to the dark hot room, where the attendant douses him several times with very hot water. The attendant accompanies him to the central hot room and swills down an area of the hot floor so that the bather can sit or lie on it. He remains here for ten minutes or more so as to induce sweating, then sweat and dirt are removed by rubbing down with a pumice stone or a rough woollen glove (*kīs*). Several times during the sweating period the bather calls the attendant from the dark room to douse him with a dipper of hot water. Finally, he goes to either a hot or temperate room and sits near a basin. There he either rubs the sweat and dirt off himself, removing the top layer of dead skin, or else he engages an attendant to do it for him. The process is completed by a careful dousing with water, adjusted to the desired temperature, from the basin, which has been cleaned out and filled with fresh water from the hot and cold pipes. Some bathers return to the central hot room and complete the cycle of sweating and rubbing a second or third time.

Others proceed with the next stage, which is a complete cleansing with a cake of soap held inside a cellular cotton glove (*līs*). After a cursory washing-off with water, the bather then moves through the central hot room to the dark hot room, where he washes his private parts and is then doused three or four times from a large dipper held by an attendant. He then leaves the hot and temperate rooms and stands on the top step leading into the changing room, where he is finally doused by an attendant with a large dipper of hot water, the water running back into a drain in the cold pool room. His towel and second cloth are brought to him; the towel is wrapped round his shoulders and he goes to his place in the changing-room, where he sits or squats, talking to the other bathers, taking *qishr* or tea or praying if it is the time of prayer. For this purpose there is usually a *miḥrāb* in the wall of the changing-room to indicate the direction of Mecca. Eventually he begins to feel cool and then dresses in preparation for his departure. Before leaving the baths he may sit for a few minutes on a seat in the outer lobby, provided for the purpose, further to adjust his body to the outside temperature while still sheltered from the wind.

Baths can be hired by the hour, and this is usually done by rich or even moderately well-to-do men in preparation for a wedding festivity, or by a group of friends before a festival.

Ḥammām Shukr, changing room. Most changing areas in the public baths are entered through a large domed room containing a cold water pool.

Ḥammām al-Sulṭān, cold pool room. Lighting in the baths is by means of small panes of glass or alabaster in the domes overhead. This room has an octagonal pool in the centre with a single jet of water.

Ḥammām al-Maydān, cold pool room. This is a large bath, built during the Ottoman period in the 10th/16th century.

Front view of a large house, (model in exhibition).

The House

The houses of five to nine storeys rise with cliff-like walls from the narrow streets to heights of from 20 to 50 metres. They are usually occupied by a single family, which could include a married son or other relative. The building techniques and decorative motifs are centuries old, due to the unchanging needs and habits of the inhabitants. Though crowded together along the street fronts, they look out behind on to large communal vegetable gardens and orchards owned by the mosques.

The lower levels are usually built of stone, sometimes to a height of thirteen metres and are often whitewashed for protection against the heavy showers that fall regularly after noon for periods of three weeks in the rainy seasons, normally April–May and August–September. The upper walls are of baked brick with relief decoration, also often whitewashed. In the case of the older houses there is a curious method of construction, following an antique tradition going back to pre-Islamic times: each facing stone slants slightly outwards and rests on a wedge made of stone chippings. The reason for this, it is believed, is to allow the central rubble core to settle without disturbing the stability of the building, but the practice is said to have gone out of use several hundred years ago. Lintels of old doors, sometimes sunk deep in the ground below the present street level, are evidence of the considerable age of some of these buildings.

The roofs are flat and waterproofed with a mixture of loam and crushed stone. They are used by the women for drying clothes, though sometimes herbs and aromatic plants are grown there in pots as well.

The inside walls are thickly plastered, so that the

Large market garden behind the houses and within the city walls of Ṣan‘ā’.

Fourth level
Eighth level
Third level
Seventh level
Second level
Sixth level
Street
First level (ground)
Fifth level
3 2 1 0 5
Metres
N

A Entrance hall
Aa Entrance hall upper level
B Lobby
C Court
Cc Court upper level
D Animal stall
E Sheep pens
F Excrement room
G Well
H Store
J Grain and fruit store
K Loading
L Grinding mills
M Personal room
N Living room
O Bathroom
P Mafraj
Q Dīwān
R Kitchen
S Terrace
T Laundry terrace
U Shaft
V Rain water
W Water cooling box
X Women's room and wardrobe

Plans and sections of a large house, (model in exhibition).

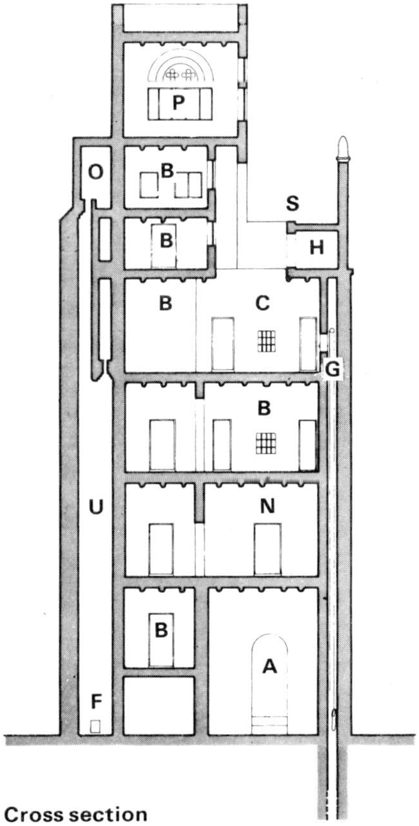

Cross section

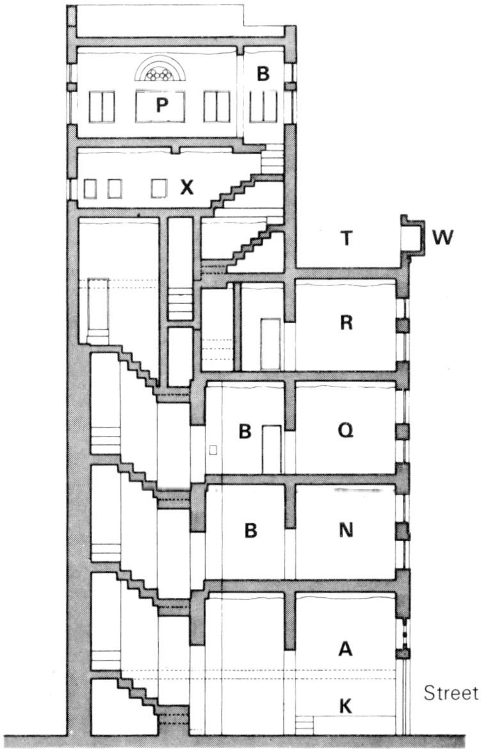

Long section

extremes of heat and cold experienced in high mountain regions are rarely felt within the house. There is no heating, although the winter climate is quite cold. The rooms are easy to ventilate because of the open screen walls which allow the wind to blow through staircases and lobbies. Ample light penetrates through the fixed fanlights made of alabaster or coloured glass held in gypsum plaster tracery. Below these fanlights there are windows almost at floor level, until recently unglazed and closed only by wooden shutters. Now many of them have glazed windows. The floors, either of stone slabs or stamped earth, are carried on wooden beams. Doors are often double, with a decorated wooden strip on the internal edge of one door; the frame is not normally decorated.

The entrance hall on the ground floor is flanked by stables for animals, usually small rooms closed with wooden doors. Cattle, sheep, goats, mules and donkeys may be kept, and sometimes a horse. There is a well, so that water can be drawn for the animals as well as the residents of the house. In small houses the grinding of flour, sesame seed and salt is carried on in the entrance hall. One or two arches cross the entrance hall to support the main internal walls and the stairs to the upper floors.

The stairs leading to the upper floors are of stone and have steep risers between 25 and 33 centimetres. The flights are short, however, and landings frequent, so that the ascent in a lofty house is not arduous. High up in the walls beside the steps there are sometimes wooden grills, which allow the women on the floors above to see who is on the stairs without being seen themselves. In large houses the central stair pier or newel is frequently as much as two metres across and may contain recesses in which guards used to squat to control movement up the stairs.

The first upper level is often a mezzanine floor, the entrance hall rising through the two storeys. It has no living-rooms but is used for storing grain and, in a large house, may include a guardroom. Wheat, corn, millet and other grain are kept in large plastered masonry bins, with walls reaching to waist level, which stand in rows down one side of each storeroom. Sometimes the querns for grinding corn are on this floor.

On the next floor are the main living rooms,

Entrance hall of a large house, (model in exhibition).

Entrance hall of another large house.

Grain storage bins on the mezzanine floor of a large house.

Stone treads of a typical staircase.

Stairs lined with decorated panels made from alabaster.

entered through a large lobby closed from the stairs by a door with a small wooden shutter. This door and the other doors of the living-rooms are frequently decorated with fine carved patterns, and are swung on hooks which hang in eyes nailed to the face of the door frame. It is therefore easy to remove them at will. In one corner of the lobby is a shaft which goes down to the well in the entrance hall and continues up through the height of the house, so that water can be drawn at any level, including that of the kitchen near the top. On the outside wall of this and all other levels is an openwork box of wood, stone or brick to contain a jar of water to cool in the wind. The boxes are closed by wooden doors on the inside. There are holes in the bottom of the projecting part to allow women to see down to the street and control access to the house. The most important room on this floor is the family living-room, into which strangers are customarily shown on social occasions or for business discussions. Adjoining it is a small room for preparing beverages and storing charcoal for the water-pipes.

Lobby outside living quarters of a large house, (model in exhibition).

Living room of a large house with black carpets and seat runners, typical of Yemen.

In the Yemen all rooms, whether they are used for eating, sitting or sleeping, or for all three functions, are furnished in the same fashion. The floor nearest the door is usually kept clear to allow shoes to be left just inside the room. Part or all of the remainder is carpeted and lined round the walls with a continuous seat of mattresses stuffed with kapok or wool and often covered with strips of carpet. Behind them, against the plastered wall, stand back-rests of vertical cushions, stuffed with a local cottony plant and covered in bright cotton cloth, and above these are sometimes placed smaller cushions to serve as head-rests, often with fringed white antimacassars. There are usually hard arm-rest bolsters stuffed with the same plant as the back rests.

In these rooms will be found the articles in every-day use: the heavy brass mortar in which spices and coffee beans are pounded; the brass ewers from which water is poured; the tinned-brass coffee pots, and the small white handleless cups from which coffee is drunk. These cups are now imported from China and are sometimes kept in a basketwork container with a conical lid decorated with cowries. Incense is burned, particularly on special occasions, in tinned-brass or copper containers or in earthenware pots. Lighting before the introduction of electricity was by wicks floating in sesame oil in open copper lamps or in stone or alabaster bowls with spouts for wicks.

Bathroom in a large house.

On this floor there is the lavatory-bathroom. The walls and floor are coated with a mixture of lime and alabaster which can be washed without difficulty. The 'long-drop' type of latrine consists of a square stone platform with a hole opening into a vertical shaft which runs down to a chamber at street level, in which the dry excrement is collected and eventually used as fuel in the public baths. The square platform has a sloping section in front, which leads liquid down to a channel in the stone floor from which it passes through an opening in the outside wall to run down a vertical drainage surface on the outer face of the building. Frequently these drains are elegantly shaped and decorated. As soon as it reaches the ground the liquid disappears into an underground drainage sump. Liquids are not led into the latrine shaft or chamber below; as Ṣan'ā' has a low humidity, the excrement dries very quickly. One washes oneself squatting on a pair of square stones in front of a stone cylinder on which stands a container of water. Sometimes there is a large earthenware jar in one corner of the bathroom.

Above the main living-rooms is the *dīwān*, the reception-room, used by both men and women for family celebrations such as births and weddings.

The floor above the *dīwān* contains the smaller rooms used by women and children, and the kitchen. The kitchen is a smoke-darkened room with a masonry-built stove, over which the ceiling is often raised, or there may be a series of chimneys emerging on the roof. Surplus

Dīwān of a large house, more than 300 years old, with men smoking water-pipes.

Dīwān of another large house over 300 years old.

Kitchen showing cooking stove and store for utensils next to it.

smoke from coals in the stove finds its way out through the northern, western and southern walls of the house, which are pierced with a large number of holes arranged in patterns.

The stove consists of a block of masonry with a row of three or four holes, lined with vertical earthenware cylinders; access is provided at the base of each cylinder so that hot coals can be inserted or taken out during cooking. The walls of the stove are packed with ash to provide insulation. There is a raised washing surface with a drain through and down the outside wall. Adjoining it there may be a masonry bench for the preparation of food. A push quern for grinding salt and herbs stands on the floor and has to be used in a squatting position.

There is normally only one kitchen in a house, however large, and it is shared by all the women. There are several reasons why the kitchen is usually two floors above the living-room; the seclusion of women; the need to

Kitchen, showing sink and ventilation.

serve refreshment up to the *mafraj*, the principal room for entertainment, as well as down to the *dīwān*; and, most important, a desire to keep the smoke and fumes away from the windows of the living-rooms as much as possible. Kitchen chimneys are placed on the north side of the *mafraj*, where there are no open windows.

Cooking by traditional methods is a laborious business. Wood is scarce and expensive, so animal dung, made into flat cakes and dried in the sun, is used as fuel. Nowadays electricity and imported fuels are available, but the old fuel is still used in many houses and in nearby villages.

Stone bowls of various shapes and sizes are employed in the preparation of dishes. Other kitchen utensils are clay pots and jugs and tinned-copper containers with lids.

The Yemeni cuisine is frugal, with cereals as the staple food. Many kinds of bread are made from various grains including wheat, barley, sorghum, lentils and other legumes. The finest is the wheat bread, *khubz*. When the slightly leavened dough has risen it is divided into small balls. The ball of dough is then worked and stretched across the *makhbazah*, a sort of pillow mounted on a basket-work frame, which serves to press the flap-jack on to the inside of the hot 'oven' or *tannūr* – an earthenware cylinder in which a fire has been lit. Dishes made from wheat bread include *sūsī*, in which the *khubz* is combined with eggs and clarified butter, and *sabāyā*, where a shortened bread is served with clarified butter and honey; they are cooked in stoneware dishes on the top of the *tannūr*. For heavier breads, such as those of barley and sorghum, the ball of dough is not stretched on the *makhbazah* but is simply spread with both hands on the side of the hot *tannūr*. Types of porridge include the staple food of the countryside, *'aṣīd*, made from sorghum flour, and *harīsh*, made from crushed wheat. These may be eaten with milk gruel, meat broth, clarified butter or, in the case of *harīsh*, honey. A light spongy pancake, *laḥūḥ*, is also made from slightly soured sorghum dough and cooked on a griddle or *ṣulā'*.

Meat and milk gruels were always important items in the diet, but in traditional cooking few vegetables were

Cooking with stone vessel; pots of coffee on cylindrical oven/stove.

Bread inside hot oven (*tannūr*).

used. Until the second Turkish occupation in the latter part of the last century, onions, peppers and white radishes were the only common vegetables. The standard main course for lunch is *ḥilbah*, which is made from the ground seeds of fenugreek, twice soaked in water to rid them of their natural bitterness and then beaten to a white froth. This is flavoured with ground spring onions, hot peppers, mint and spices, and served with meat broth in a heated stone dish. During the meal the diners add to the *ḥilbah* from other dishes, stirring the mixture and scooping it up with their bread. Meat or chicken, which is usually boiled in clay pots or tinned copper cauldrons, is served as the last course of the meal.

At the top of the house is the *mafraj*, a long room with wide shuttered openings for windows on three sides that give extensive views over the housetops and the country and are embellished with fine stucco work. The fitted upper windows have rich stucco tracery and coloured glass. At one end is a lobby, separated from the *mafraj* by double folding doors, which are usually opened when the room is in use to permit a view through the lobby windows. These penthouse rooms do not occur in the oldest houses in Ṣan'ā' – those which are considered to be more than three hundred years old. In them the place for recreation was provided by three rooms at the top of the building. The *mafraj* is the principal room for entertaining visitors and contains the finest possessions of the family. These are often laid on tinned copper trays, decorated with incised geometric and floral patterns, sometimes with three legs.

The recreational activities carried on in the *mafraj* are the smoking of the water-pipe (*mada'ah*) and the chewing of *qāt*, which is a widespread custom in southern Arabia. *Qāt* is a small fresh leaf, bought in bunches and chewed as a stimulant. The leaf is not swallowed but is kept in the mouth, and while it is being chewed frequent draughts of water are drunk from jars which have been perfumed by the smoke of frankincense (*lubān*) and other perfumes. The furniture of the *mafraj* includes three or four water-pipes. The ancillary equipment, consisting of an ornate box for tobacco, a brazier for charcoal to light the pipe and a receptacle for the dottle when the pipe is finished, would be kept in the lobby. Spittoons shaped like hour-glasses are provided for the *qāt* chewers to dispose of the refuse of the *qāt*. In some old houses there are magnificent candle stands (*sham'dān*) decorated with figured scenes and dedicatory inscriptions in silver on brass. The floors are covered with Mashriqī rugs, black with white borders, 94 centimetres wide and 3.9 to 7.7 metres long, or Bīshah rugs, with orange, red and purple stripes, 84 centimetres wide and 3.7 metres long.

View of a *mafraj*.

Another view of same room. The *mafraj* in the exhibition is based on this.

Mafraj of a house of recent construction. The lacquer doors include a hurricane lamp in their decoration.

Men dancing in a *mafraj*.

Manẓar with musical instruments being played. In the foreground a typical stand for Yemeni coffee, made of coffee husk (*qishr*) and ginger.

Girl having her feet painted with henna.

Costume

Traditional costume incorporated elements that served to mark an individual's social status and, in theory, every group in the social hierarchy had a distinctive dress. There is, however, little reliable evidence that such intricacies were in fact ever fully observed. Successful individuals of the lower groups often omitted elements which they regarded as demeaning in the dress prescribed for them, and adopted others worn by groups of higher status. Yet, to over-emphasize the importance of individual social advancement or even eccentricity would give a false picture of traditional society. For, in spite of the formal Islamic ethos of the religious equality of all believers, there existed a variant tradition wherein men are not equal in this world, nor even potentially equal, but inherently unequal. In such a world social concord was based, not upon tolerance among different though equal individuals, but upon the maintenance of division, of distance between different and unequal groups. In this environment clothing served as a chosen marker of social identity.

There was a well-known and crucial division, marked by dress, between Muslims and non-Muslims, so that Jews, Christians and Hindus were prohibited from wearing the costume of Muslims. But divisions among the Muslims were also marked by dress: differences of political organization, tribal versus non-tribal; of rank in the hierarchy of occupations and descent groups (e.g., a descendant of the Prophet, or a member of a despised profession, such as a butcher); and of age, the minor and the adult having somewhat different clothing.

For instance, the model of the *'ālim*, a religious scholar or descendant of a family with a tradition of learning, wears a narrow-sleeved full-length robe (*zinnah*), a waistcoat (*ṣudayrī*), another full-length robe (*qamīṣ*) with very wide long sleeves, a wide-sleeved smooth wool overcoat (*jūkh*), a fine silverwork dagger (*thūmah*) worn at an angle on a rich cloth belt, and, over his shoulder, a heavy cloth of striped design woven with silver thread (*maṣnaf*). On his head he wears an *ʿimāmah*, comprising a white sweat-cap (*maʿraqah*), a stiff black felt cap (*qāwaq Thulāʾī*) with an embroidered top (*qiḥf*), and finally a white cloth which is wound round and round and can be as much as six metres long (*shāsh*). This costume includes several imported materials, whereas prior to the twentieth century, when such imports were far more difficult to obtain, locally dyed indigo cotton cloth was used by all classes.

Event at its finest, the clothing of a tribesman is less elaborate than the costume described above. Over a simpler *zinnah* he wears a wide-sleeved robe of indigo-dyed cotton (*qamīṣ muṣabbagh*), a dagger (*ʿasīb*) erect on a leather belt, a shoulder cloth (*liḥfah*) of lighter weight than the *maṣnaf*, woven in brightly striped cotton, and on his head a turban of indigo dyed cotton cloth (*qubʿ*).

Unlike the cumbersome *qamīṣ* of the tribesman, the dress of the labourer consists of an unsewn piece of cloth (*maqṭab*) wrapped around the waist as a skirt, held with a strip of cloth or, more recently, a leather belt (*kamar*), and a shirt with an open front made in the style of the traditional *madraʿah* in indigo-dyed cotton.

Female costume exhibits a different form of social distinction. While a man's costume reflects his public role in Muslim society, a woman's dress does not contain specific marks of the status of her descent group. On the other hand, her dress, in particular the veil, symbolizes her isolation from public life. It illustrates the duality of her status, unequal but protected; she does not openly contend for her needs or proclaim her status on the public scene. The veil is generally worn in the city, but tribeswomen do not usually wear it.

Within the family, the change from child to adult is marked with little ceremony. The boy acquires adult clothing, essentially the headgear and the dagger, about the age of puberty; the girl exchanges her bonnet (*qarqūsh*) for a woman's headgear at the time of her marriage. However, she has begun to veil sometime before she reaches the minimum age for marriage, which is nine years.

The girl's face panel, as exhibited, is of an older type, the *burqaʿ* with holes for the eyes, which was common for girls until the early 1950s. According to those who dye the contemporary women's face panel, the red, white and black *maghmūq*, the *burqaʿ* was abandoned sometime about the turn of the century. Even within the home a woman should veil from all men except those who fall within the prohibited degrees. These rules are relaxed only with the very young and the very old. The indoor veil (*lithmah*) is formed of a single long rectangular cloth, ingeniously wrapped so as to cover all but the eyes.

In contrast to their outdoor dress, women's costume at their gatherings and festivities is brilliant and even ostentatious. Women of Ṣanʿā' go out almost every day to women's parties, the most important of which are the celebrations on the occasion of a marriage, which occupy about twenty days in all, and those marking the forty-day resting period of a mother after the birth of her child. For such gatherings all women of status wear the *ʿuṣbah* head-dress. A full *ʿuṣbah* comprises more than ten articles. On a bride's wedding night and at some of the celebrations following the consummation of her marriage, she wears a hired gold *tashbīk* head-dress, mounted by the marriage attendant, the *shāriʿah.* On such occasions the *shāriʿah* paints the hands and feet of the bride and of her chosen guests and friends with henna.

Girl having her hands painted with henna.

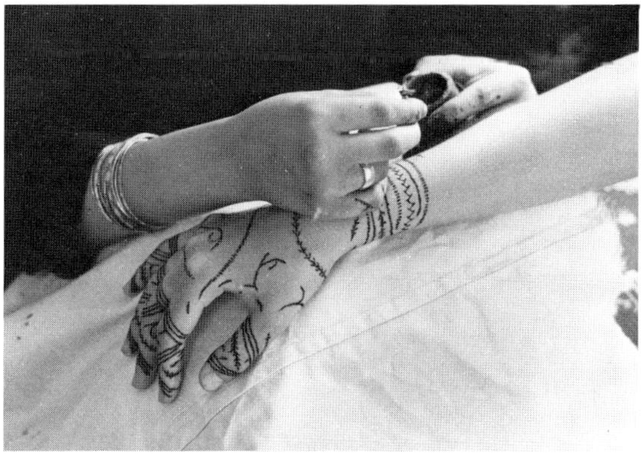

Selected Exhibits

Iron padlock and key. Made in Ṣa'dah. Shown open and closed.

Wooden door-lock, back and front.

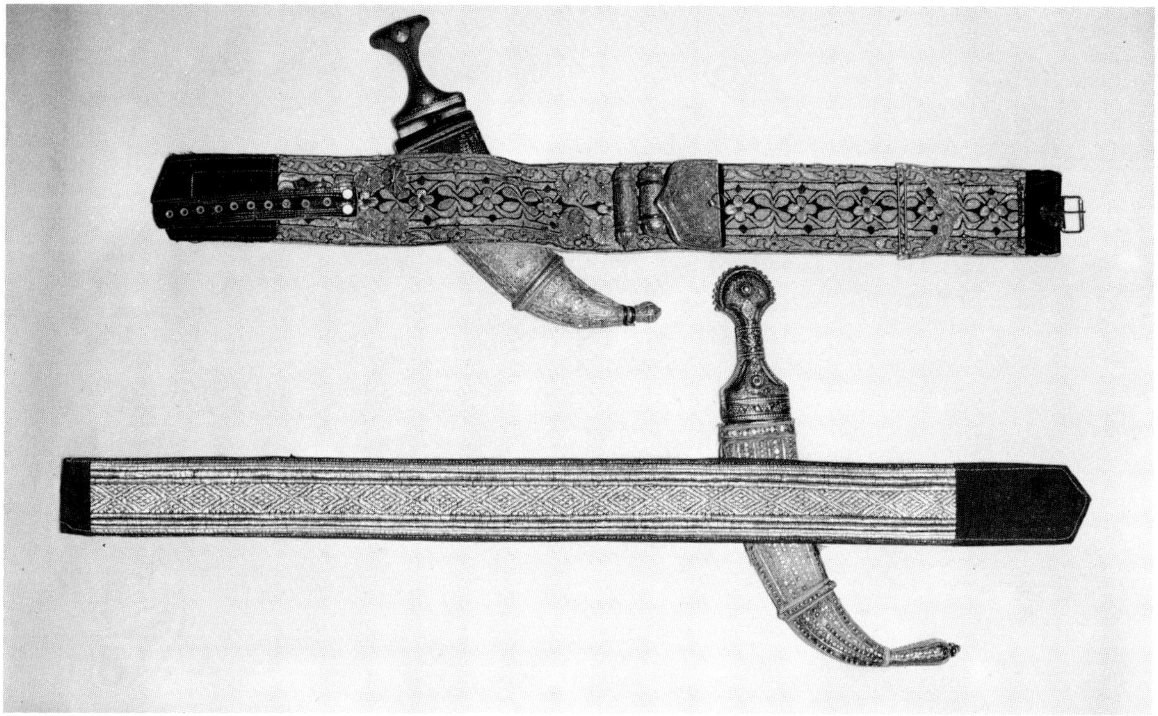

Daggers with embroidered belts.

Steelyard with two hooks and tray. Gradated in units of 4, 8 and 16 (16 units = 7in).

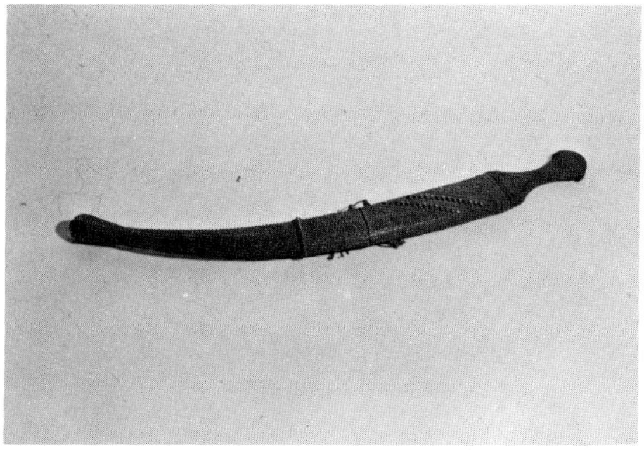

Dagger with silver mount. Crescent shaped pommel with silver-gilt ornament.

Carved bracket from the Great Mosque at Ṣan'ā'.

Brass mosque lamp with eight spouts and chain for suspension. Yemen, 6th–9th/12th–15th century.

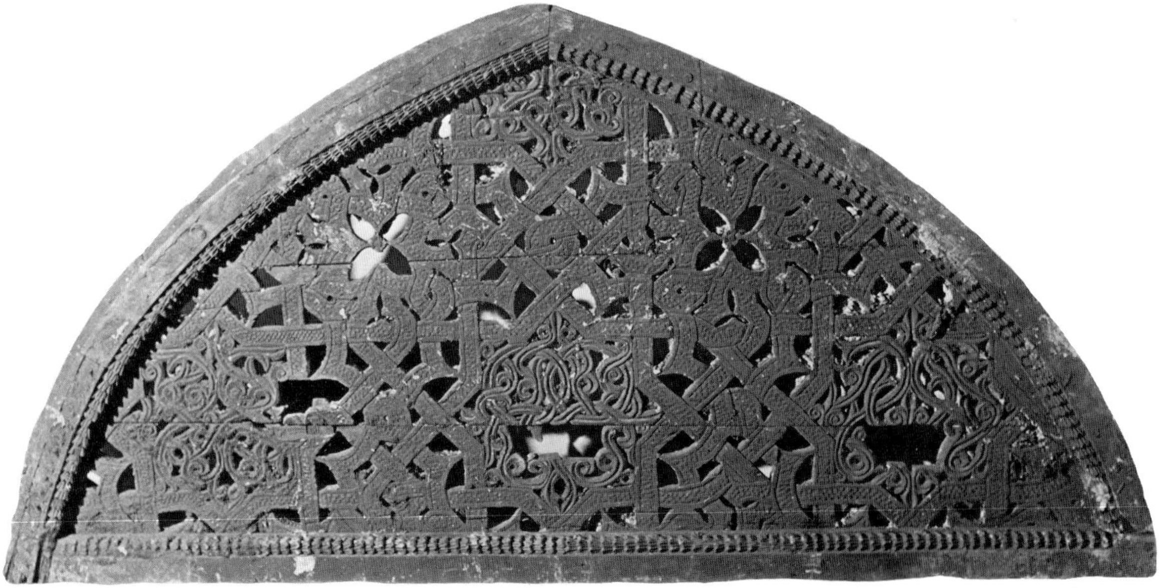

Carved tympanum from Great Mosque. 3rd or 4th/9th or 10th century.

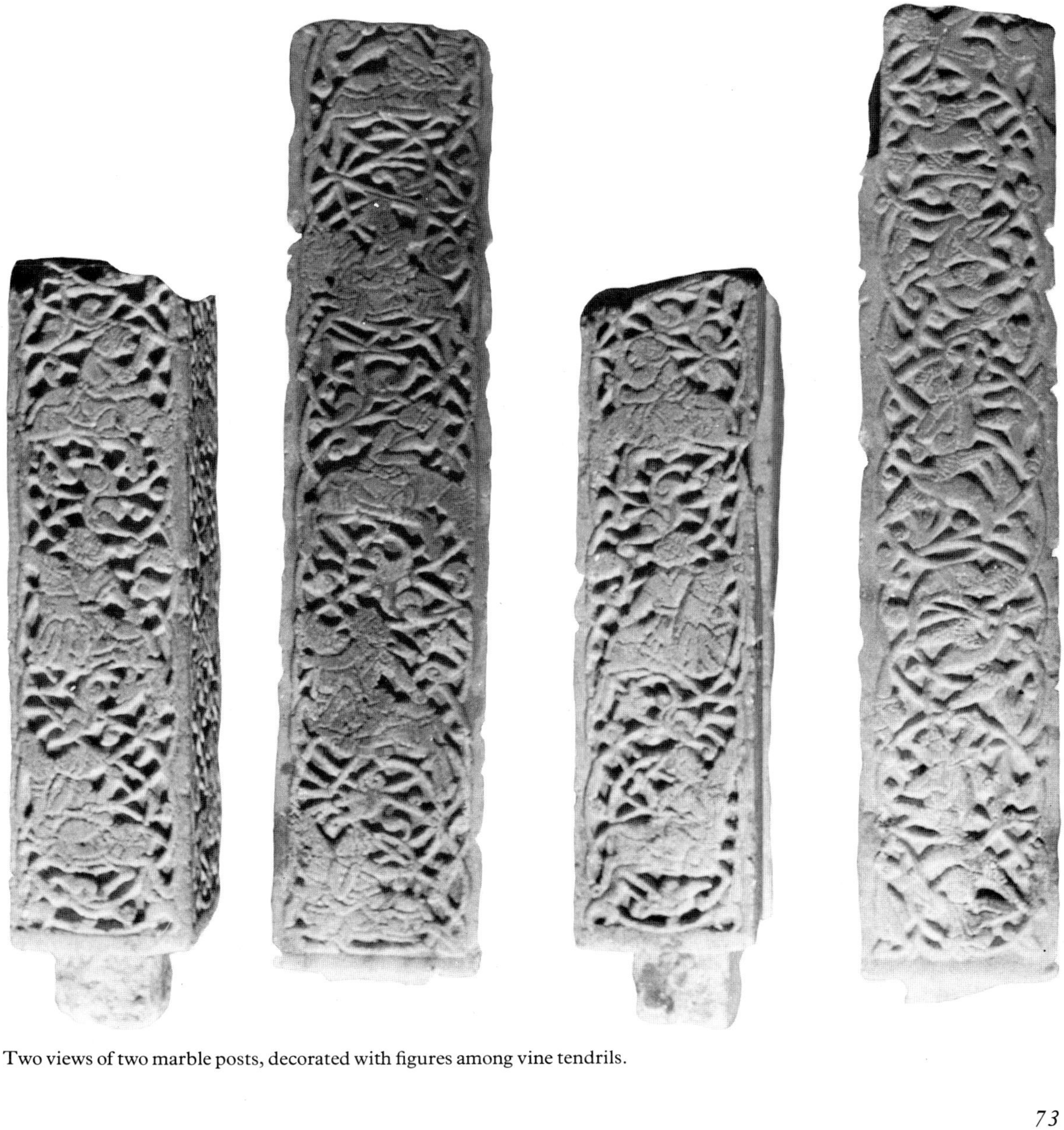

Two views of two marble posts, decorated with figures among vine tendrils.

Silver finial from 7th/13th century tomb of Shaykh Aḥmad ibn 'Alwan at Yifrus near Ṭā'izz. Inscribed with date 1179 H.

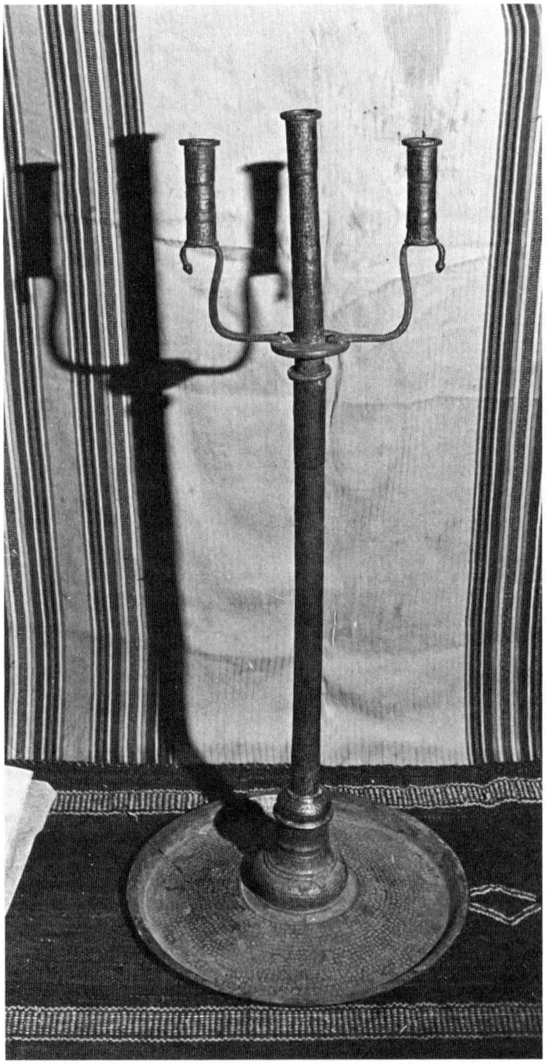

Three branched tinned copper candlestick made in three sections.

Student's stone mosque lamp with eleven spouts for wicks.

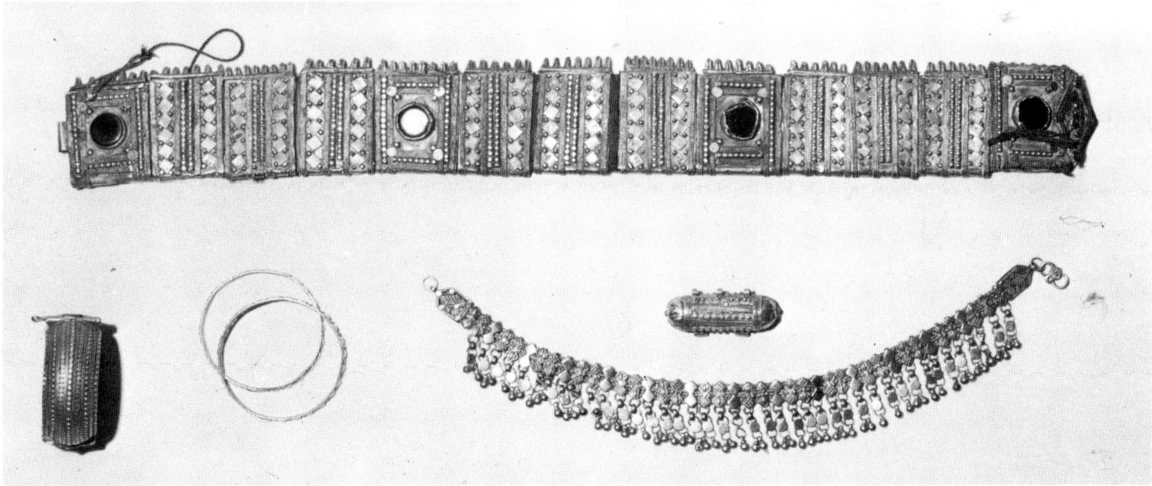

Silver ornaments for women.

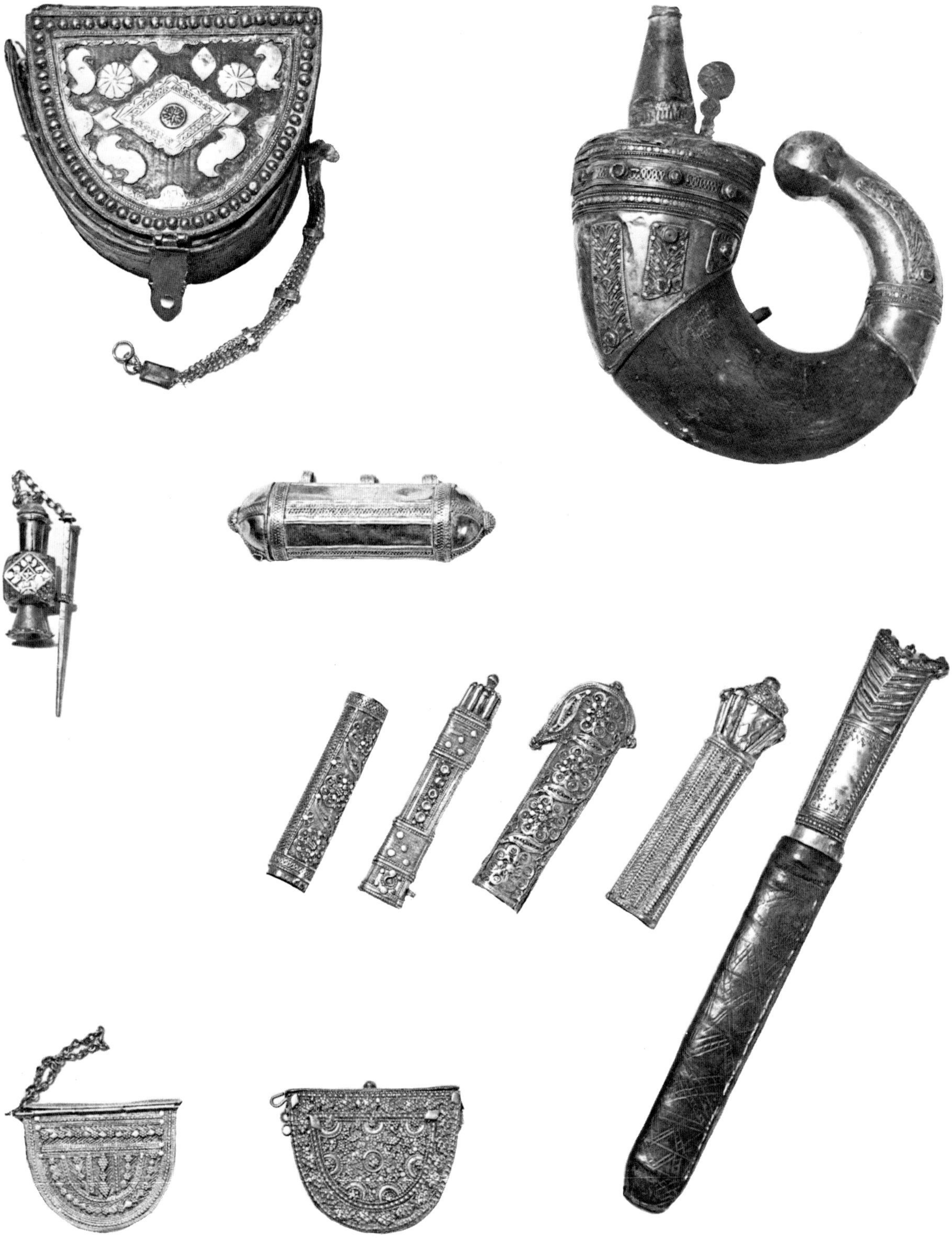

Silver and silver-mounted articles of male dress.

Candle-stand and detail showing inscription and floral decoration.

Making bread using the *makhbazah*, a kind of cushion made from palm fronds and cotton.

Water-pipe with celadon bowl encased in brass with silver ornament. Typical of Ṣan'ā' workmanship.

Water-pipe with brass bowl and pewter base.
Perhaps Hyderabad work, 11th–12th/17th–18th century.

Candle-stands with decoration and inscriptions.

Incense-burner (tinned copper) in form of a pavilion, (unavailable for exhibition).

Copper and brass bowls with decorative and geometric motifs.

Wooden chest with overall decoration of semi-precious stones and glass, (unavailable for exhibition).

Copper plate with Yemeni poems. 10th/16th century.

Candle-stand, silver on brass with musicians and dancers in cartouches.

Brass ewers, one with plaques on both sides and fluted lid, incised 'Muḥammad'.

Silver cup with blazon. 7th–8th/13th–14th century.

Incense burner (earthenware) in form of a house.

Tobacco box inlaid with mother-of-pearl.

Spittoons of turned brass with floreate decoration.

Folding lantern with decorative pierced copper top and bottom and cloth sides.

Red and black lacquer boxes.

Bibliography

Books on the Yemen of general interest in European languages; for special studies and historical texts, see Macro 1960 (up to 1960) and Serjeant and Lewcock 1976 for later publications.

Bidwell, R. L., *Travellers in Arabia*, London 1976.

Bury, G. W., *Arabia Infelix: or the Turks in Yemen*, London 1915.

Fayein, C., *A French Doctor in the Yemen*, London 1957.

Great Britain: Admiralty, Naval Intelligence Division, *Western Arabia and the Red Sea* (B.R. 527: Geographical Handbook Series), London 1946.

Hansen, Thorkild, *Arabia Felix*, London 1964.

Harris, W. B., *A Journey through the Yemen*, Edinburgh 1893.

Hogarth, D. G., *The penetration of Arabia, a record of the development of western knowledge concerning the Arabian Peninsula*, London 1905.

Ingrams, H., *The Yemen: Imams, rulers and revolutions*, London 1963.

Kay, H. C., *Yaman: its early mediaeval history*, London 1892 (reprint London 1970).

Khazraji, 'Alī b. al-Ḥasan, *The pearl-strings; a history of the Resuliyy dynasty of the Yemen*, ed. by M. Asal and trans. by J. W. Redhouse, London 1906–8.

Kiernan, R. H., *The unveiling of Arabia; the story of Arabian travel and discovery*, London 1937 (reprint Beirut 1971).

Macro, E., *Bibliography of Yemen and notes on Mocha*, Coral Gables, Fla., USA, 1960.

Manzoni, R., *El-Yemen. Tre anni nell-Arabia Felice*, Rome 1884.

Müller, D. H., *Die Burgen und Schlössen Südarabiens nach dem Iklil des Hamdani*, Vienna 1879.

Niebuhr, C., *Travels through Arabia and other countries in the East*, trans. by R. Heron, Edinburgh 1792 (reprint Beirut 1969).

Phillips, Wendell, *Qataban and Sheba*, London 1955.

Playfair, R. L., *A history of Arabia Felix or Yemen, from the commencement of the Christian era to the present, including an account of the British settlement at Aden*, Bombay 1859 (reprint Amsterdam 1970).

Rihani, Amin, *Arabian Peak and Desert*, London 1930.

Rossi, Z., *El-Yemen*, Turin 1927.

Scott, H., *In the High Yemen*, London 1942.

Serjeant, R. B., *The Portuguese off the South Arabian Coast. Ḥadramī chronicles with Yemeni and European accounts of Dutch pirates off Mocha in the seventeenth century*, Oxford 1963.

Serjeant, R. B. and Lewcock, R. B., *Ṣan'ā', an Islamic City*, London 1976.

Tritton, A., *Rise of the Imams of Ṣan'ā'*, London 1925.

Wavell, A., *A modern pilgrim in Mecca and a siege in Ṣan'ā'*, London 1912.

Wenner, M. W., *Modern Yemen 1918–1966*, Baltimore 1967.